This workbook belongs to: _____

# food smarts

## Kids Workbook

California's CalFresh Healthy Living, with funding from the United States Department of Agriculture's Supplemental Nutrition Assistance Program—USDA SNAP, helped produce this material. These institutions are equal opportunity providers and employers. For important nutrition information, visit https://calfresh.dss.ca.gov/cfhl.

3rd Edition

v.20220207

ISBN: 9798411394894 Full Color Interior
ISBN: 9798416112226 Black and White Interior

Some vector art included was provided by Vecteezy.com and freepik.com.
Printed in the United States of America.

# Contents

# INTRODUCTIONS

# Welcome

Food Smarts invites you to discover how to eat for you.

Your **Hunger,**

Your **Day,**

Your **Mind,**

Your **Energy,**

Your **Schedule,**

Your **Culture,**

Your **Health,**

Your **Budget,**

Your **Time,**

Your **Family,**

Your **Well-Being,**

Your **Joy.**

We encourage you to learn to ask questions, seek answers, and get support from trusted sources in your community, family, health care providers, and your Food Smarts Workshop facilitator. We hope that Food Smarts gives you the skills you need to take good care of yourself now and for your future.

*Thanks to Portion Balance Coalition, Georgetown University for this message.*

# Taste Test

★ **Describe the foods in the taste test—be as descriptive as you can!**

Touch

Smell

Sight

Sound

Taste

Texture

# Food Collage

★ **Use the art supplies on your table to create a collage about one of the topics below.**

❶ Make a collage showing different types of food such as vegetables, fruits, grains, meat, dairy and beans.

❷ Make a collage showing foods of different colors.

❸ Make a collage showing foods that are whole and foods that are processed.

❹ Make a collage showing foods you like, foods you don't like, and foods you want to try.

❺ Make a collage showing foods that keep our bodies strong.

❻ Make a collage showing what it means to be healthy or to live in a healthy community.

8

# Your Healthy Life

Imagine yourself when you are older or on your own. What would a healthy and happy life look like to you? What are you doing? Where are you? Who are you with? What words or pictures come to mind? Write or draw about it here:

# Your Healthy Goals

★ **Would you like to help your family be healthier? Would you like to do more to take care of your body? Create a SMART Goal.**

» **S**pecific—Avoid words like "more," "less" or "better."

» **M**easurable—How will you know when you've achieved it?

» **A**ction Based—Not everything is in your control; make goals that you can achieve with your actions.

» **R**ealistic—Choose goals you're likely to accomplish. Start small.

» **T**ime Frame—Set a goal to achieve this week.

---

★ *Some examples:*

» I will drink water with my lunch at school this week.

» I will ride my bike on Saturday for half an hour.

» I will help cook a meal with my family one time this week.

---

## Your Goals

| Write down several healthy practices you would like to do more often. After you've finished, circle the three things that are most important to you. | |
| --- | --- |
| In this box, rewrite the ideas you circled above as SMART goals. | 1. |
| | 2. |
| | 3. |

*See also Goal Tracker Handout.*

# Goal Tracker

★ **Make a healthy SMART Goal that you can work on for a few weeks.**

I will _____  _____ this week.
            (action)                                      (how often)

**To track your progress each week, ask yourself:**

» Did I achieve my goal this past week? Why or why not?

» What was challenging about my goal?

» What was easy?

» Should I continue working on this goal or create a new one? If so, what is it?

| Week (end of) | My Progress |
| --- | --- |
| 1 | |
| 2 | |
| 3 | |
| 4 | |
| 5 | |
| 6 | |

# The Leah's Pantry DO EAT Food List

★ What are your "go-to" healthy foods? Check the list below. Do you see any of your favorites?

★ ***Whole Grains & Other Complex Carbohydrates***

Some carbohydrates are "complex." They take a lot of work for your body to break down. They provide more nutrients and help you feel full longer.

*Examples: brown rice, whole wheat products (bread, tortillas), oatmeal, quinoa, amaranth, lentils, beans, starchy fruits and vegetables*

★ ***Healthy Fats***

The human body needs different kinds of fats for health. Without fat, the body cannot use some vitamins. Children's brains need healthy fats too. Fats are also slow to digest. This can help you stay full for a long time. Choose fats that have been minimally or not at all processed.

*Examples: avocados, whole nuts and nut butters (low-salt or unsalted), peanuts and peanut butter, olives and olive oil, seeds, fatty fish like salmon and sardines*

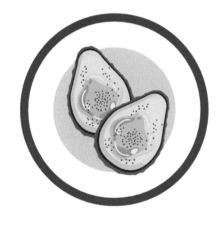

★ ***Colorful Vegetables***

Different colored vegetables and fruits have different nutrients. To get a variety, try to "eat the rainbow" every day. Enjoy them raw and cooked in different ways, too. Enjoy leafy greens as often as possible.

*[continues on next page...]*

### ★ Whole Fruits

Whole, fresh fruits contain natural sugars in small amounts. These sugars give quick energy and have vitamins, minerals, and fiber. Choose colorful fruits. Enjoy them raw or minimally cooked.

### ★ Protein from Plants

Whether you're a vegetarian or not, enjoy some protein from plants. These foods often have more fiber and less saturated fat than foods that come from animals. They can also be cheaper and last longer.

*Examples: beans, lentils, nuts and nut butters, seeds and seed butters, tofu and tempeh*

### ★ Healthy Beverages

Water is the perfect drink for a healthy body. If you want something else for a change, drink beverages made with clean water, unsweetened milk or milk substitutes, and whole, natural foods. They can be flavored with fruits, herbs, spices or vanilla extract.

*Examples: water flavored with fresh fruit, iced or hot herbal teas, unsweetened milk and milk substitutes (i.e. almond, soy)*

 Can you make a SMART Goal about adding one of these foods to your diet? For recipe ideas, check EatFresh.org.

# Weight and Body Size

A healthy weight and body size look different for everyone. Each body's natural weight setpoint is different and depends on a lot of factors—many of them outside of our control. Remember, your health is more than just your weight. All bodies deserve to be treated with love, regardless of weight and size.

Many times, conversations about healthy bodies focus exclusively on calories, body size, and food choices. However, there are many other important and joyful ways to care for our bodies that also improve our confidence, strength, and energy.

» moving your body as much as you can—even for short bursts during the day

» paying attention to how certain foods impact our mood and energy levels

» getting a good night's sleep

» exposing our bodies to nature and sunshine

» noticing when media images and advertisements promote negative thoughts about your own body—feel free to block them!

» giving appreciation for what your body can do

» giving and getting physical touch and affection, like hugs

## How do I lose weight?

Have you ever asked yourself this question? Wanting to lose weight can be a normal desire; however, losing weight doesn't necessarily make us healthier or happier. Many weight-loss approaches encourage a too restrictive diet and lifestyle that are difficult to maintain long term. Over time, they may also slow down your metabolism and hurt your relationship with food and your body. When trying to lose weight, use an approach that you can sustain for the future. Remember to listen to your body and honor your hunger, fullness, and appetite.

If you are seeking more individual guidance in this area, seek advice from a registered dietitian who can work with you more closely to build a healthy relationship with food and support you in your health goals.

# Cooking with EatFresh.org

### ★ Where do you find trustworthy nutritional information online?

EatFresh.org makes shopping and home cooking easy. Go to www.EatFresh.org right now and start exploring!

» Find healthy, inexpensive, and quick recipes.

» Print, save, share, and text recipes to your mobile phone.

» Learn lifestyle tips to keep you healthy and feeling your best.

» Ask a question to the EatFresh.org dietitian.

» Save time planning and shopping with meal plans.

» Apply for SNAP/CalFresh.

» Learn basic cooking skills and how to substitute ingredients to use what you already have at home.

» View the website in multiple languages.

» View nutritional information for each recipe.

COOKING

# Kitchen Safety

⭐ **Read these helpful rules to stay safe when having fun in the kitchen.**

**1** Small children should not use sharp knives. Keep them out of reach and out of sight.

**2** Always turn off the stove and oven when done. Even when turned off, it can still be hot and dangerous.

**3** Make sure all handles on pots and pans are turned so that they are not sticking out—this avoids accidentally knocking a pot off the stove.

**4** Cook hot soup or hot food on a back burner if possible.

**5** Be clean!

> » Always use clean hands—to make sure you have clean hands, wash them in hot, soapy water for at least 20 seconds (or for the amount of time it takes to sing the ABCs).

> » Clean countertops and dishes well before and after cooking.

> » Always clean items that touched raw meats and eggs right away. Don't put cooked food on a plate or surface that was touched by raw foods!

**6** Although it's tempting, avoid licking mixing spoons or fingers—taste it when it is done cooking, or use a clean spoon each time.

**7** Keep electronic appliances away from water.

**8** Put ingredients back after using.

**9** Always have an adult around to supervise!

*Information adapted from kids-cooking-activities.com*

# Glossary of Recipe Terms

## ★ Do you know your cooking words?

Connect each term at left to its definition at right.

### ★ *Food Prep*

|  |  |
|------|------------|
| chop | to rub food on a grater to make shreds |
| dice | to cut solid food into chunks or medium-sized pieces |
| grate | to pre-mix food with wet or dry seasonings; helps develop the flavor as well as moisturize it |
| julienne | to chop into extremely small pieces |
| knead | to cut solid food into small cubes of the same size |
| marinate | to cut food into thin strips |
| mince | to remove the skin of fruits or vegetables |
| peel | to press dough (i.e. for bread) repeatedly with hands |
| puree | to beat quickly, in order to add air and volume to food |
| whip/whisk | to blend until smooth |

### ★ *Cooking*

|  |  |
|------|------------|
| bake | to cook/brown food in a small amount of hot oil |
| boil | to cook slowly in liquid over low heat, with bubbles barely forming on the surface |
| broil | to cook with medium heat, usually in an oven |
| deep fry | to cook with steam, usually in a closed container |
| fry | to cook over direct heat |
| grill | to cook in a deep layer of very hot oil |
| roast | to heat a liquid until the surface bubbles continuously |
| sauté | to cook in very hot oil |
| simmer | to cook with medium-high heat, usually in an oven |
| steam | to cook under strong and direct heat |

# How to Read a Recipe

★ **Have you ever tried to make something that came out all wrong? Reading a recipe can help.**

## Smoothies
Prep Time: 5 min   Cook Time: 0 min   Yield: 2 servings

**Ingredients:**
» 4 frozen strawberries
» 1 cup low-fat plain yogurt
» ½ cup 100% orange juice
» 1 banana, cut into chunks
» 4 ice cubes

**Directions:**
» Place all ingredients in a blender.
» Cover and process until smooth.

**Per 1 Cup Serving:** 150 calories, 2g total fat (1g sat), 30g carb, 2g fiber, 65mg sodium

**1** Read the recipe well before starting.

» Make sure you have all the items you need and enough time for the recipe.

» Look up any words you don't know.

» When an ingredient is *optional* or *if desired*, you don't have to use it unless you want to.

» If necessary, preheat the oven while you prepare.

**2** Prepare ingredients for the recipe.

» If a recipe calls for chopped onion, for example, do the chopping now.

**3** Measure carefully.

» It helps to know abbreviations: **c.** = cup, **T.** or **tbsp**. = tablespoon, **t.** or **tsp**. = teaspoon. It's also helpful to know measurement shortcuts. For example:

4 tablespoons = ¼ cup

3 teaspoons = 1 tablespoon

**4** Pay attention to the order of the steps.

**5** If you change your recipe as you cook, make a note. That way you can prepare the dish exactly the same way next time—or not!

20

# Superstar Ingredients

★ Do you like to cook? Which of these healthy ingredients would you like to add to your menu?

## Olive Oil

**Benefits:** Olive oil helps control blood sugar and reduces inflammation.

**Uses:** Daily! Best for lower-heat cooking. Coat veggies and meat for sautéing or baking. Make salad dressing: mix 3 parts olive oil with 1 part citrus juice or vinegar.

## Salmon and Other Cold-Water Fish

**Benefits:** Omega-3 fatty acids improve brain health and protect against inflammation and heart disease.

**Uses:** Bake or broil in the oven with a little olive oil, salt, and pepper. Note that canned fish is an easy, less-expensive option often with similar nutritional benefits to fresh fish.

## Spices like Cinnamon, Ginger, Chile

**Benefits:** Some spices have health-promoting qualities. Cinnamon can help lower cholesterol and blood sugar. Ginger can help with digestion.

**Uses:** Add to anything for a little extra spice, from baked apples to curry.

## Unsalted Nuts and Seeds

**Benefits:** Nuts provide healthy fats, vitamins, and minerals that decrease your risk of diabetes and help manage your blood sugar and weight.

**Uses:** Eat as a snack, top salads and stews, add to yogurt, or try different nut or seed butters.

## Berries

**Benefits:** Berries are full of cancer-fighting nutrients, and lower the risk of heart disease and cancer.

**Uses:** Eat as a snack, add to yogurt or cereal. Note that frozen berries are an inexpensive, easy way to enjoy berries all year round.

## Green Veggies

**Benefits:** Calcium, folic acid, and vitamin K help keep bones strong and protect against heart disease. They're full of fiber!

**Uses:** Steam and drizzle with olive oil or salad dressing. Chop and toss with olive oil and garlic, then sauté or roast at 425° for about 10 minutes or until soft.

## Garlic

**Benefits:** Garlic lowers cholesterol and helps regulate blood sugar and blood pressure. It also supports a strong immune system.

**Uses:** Add minced, fresh garlic to soups, stews, stir-fries, and sauce. Add powdered garlic (not garlic salt) with butter or oil to mashed potatoes, cooked noodles, or couscous.

eatFresh

EatFresh.org contains hundreds of recipes using the above ingredients.

# Setting the Table and Eating Together

⭐ What's your favorite thing about eating with friends and family? What can make meal times special? Try these ideas for setting up a nice space and creating an enjoyable mealtime.

» Set the table or set up a buffet with utensils, plates, napkins and cups, and if you would like, add something beautiful like flowers, a table cloth, or decorations.

» Start your meal with a deep breath, a song, a poem or prayer, holding hands or just a simple thank you to the cook and helpers.

» Wait for everyone to be seated before eating.

» Ask to pass food instead of grabbing or reaching across the table.

» Do not talk with a mouth full of food.

» Use "may I please be excused," "please" and "thank you."

» Clear your plate and help clear the table after dinner.

» Eat together, put away screens, and talk about your day or tell a story!

**TRY IT!** Sometimes it's fun to set the table like you might see it in a restaurant.

» Fork to the left.

» Plate center one inch from edge of table.

» Knife and spoon to the right.

» Knife blade facing toward the plate.

» Napkin under fork or on top of plate.

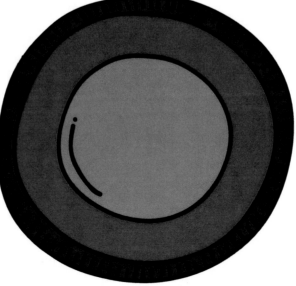

22

# CREATING A BALANCED MEAL

# What's On MyPlate?

★ What food groups do you know? Write or draw an example for each of the five food groups shown below.

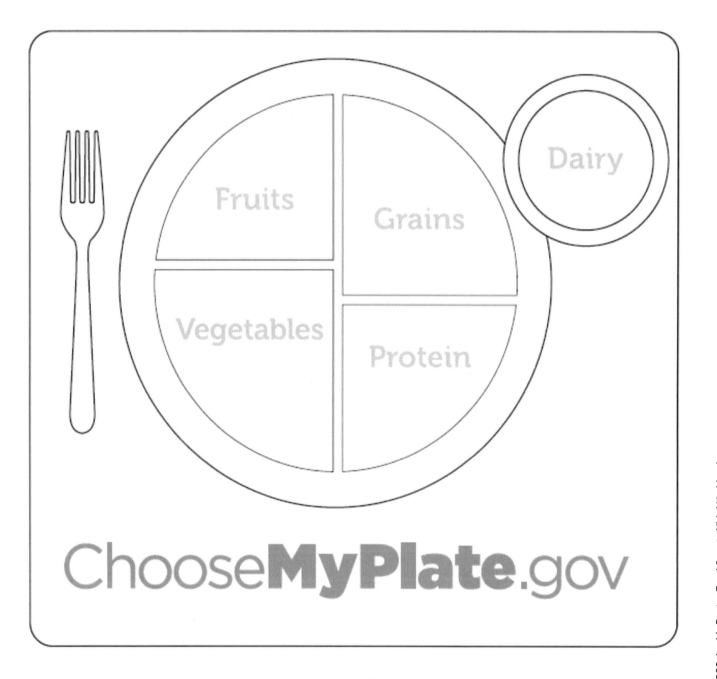

# What's On MyPlate?

★ What is your favorite meal? Write or draw it below.

ChooseMyPlate.gov

# MyPlate

★ What does a balanced diet look like? You might be familiar with this model from the USDA. What kinds of foods fall in each category?

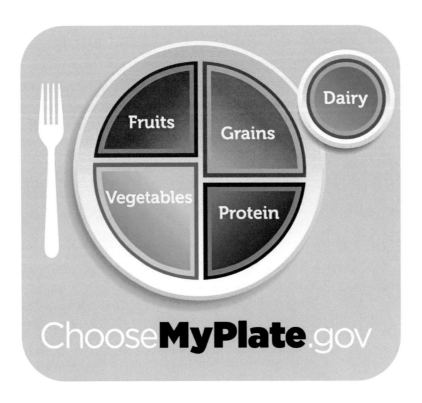

MyPlate recommends that we:

1. Fill half our plate with fruits and vegetables.

2. Eat a different kinds of vegetables—dark green as well as other colors, leafy and starchy.

3. Eat whole fruits.

4. Make half of our grains whole grains.

5. Vary our protein sources to include beans and peas, tofu, nuts seafood, eggs, and lean meats.

6. Choose foods and beverages with less added sugars, saturated fats, and sodium.

7. Consume low-fat or fat-free dairy milk or yogurt (or fortified non-dairy versions).

» What are some ways you already or plan to follow these recommendations?

» What can be challenging for you when following these recommendations?

» How would you adapt this model to fit your culture, religious practices or food preferences?

Source: www.dietaryguidelines.gov

# Healthy Eating Plate

★ Compare MyPlate to Healthy Eating Plate. How are they alike and different?

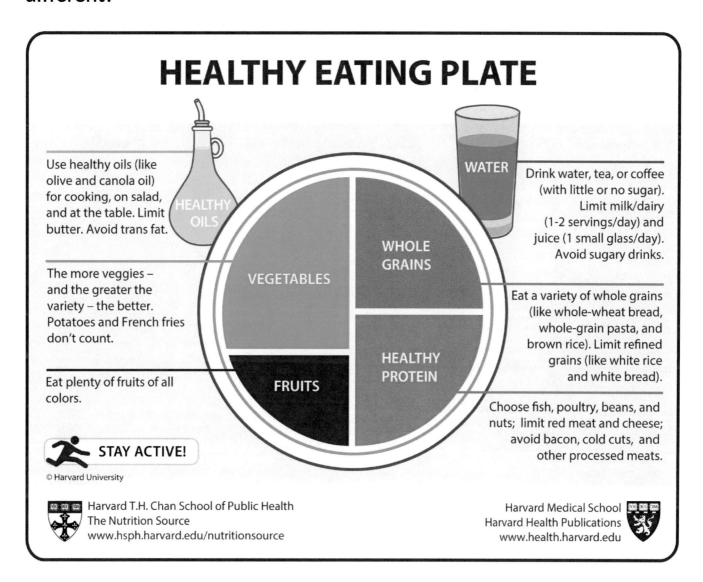

## HEALTHY EATING PLATE

**HEALTHY OILS** — Use healthy oils (like olive and canola oil) for cooking, on salad, and at the table. Limit butter. Avoid trans fat.

**VEGETABLES** — The more veggies – and the greater the variety – the better. Potatoes and French fries don't count.

**FRUITS** — Eat plenty of fruits of all colors.

**STAY ACTIVE!**

© Harvard University

**WATER** — Drink water, tea, or coffee (with little or no sugar). Limit milk/dairy (1-2 servings/day) and juice (1 small glass/day). Avoid sugary drinks.

**WHOLE GRAINS** — Eat a variety of whole grains (like whole-wheat bread, whole-grain pasta, and brown rice). Limit refined grains (like white rice and white bread).

**HEALTHY PROTEIN** — Choose fish, poultry, beans, and nuts; limit red meat and cheese; avoid bacon, cold cuts, and other processed meats.

Harvard T.H. Chan School of Public Health
The Nutrition Source
www.hsph.harvard.edu/nutritionsource

Harvard Medical School
Harvard Health Publications
www.health.harvard.edu

# Food Group Bingo

★ Listen for examples of foods. As each food is called out, write the name of the food in the box that matches the food group. For example, write apple in the box for fruit. Try to make a complete row in any direction!

| B | I | N | G | O |
|---|---|---|---|---|
| Dairy | Protein | Vegetable | Fruit | Grain |
| Combination | Fruit | Dairy | Protein | Vegetable |
| Fruit | Grain | FREE | Combination | Protein |
| Dairy | Protein | Vegetable | Fruit | Grain |
| Combination | Vegetable | Dairy | Protein | Vegetable |

# Make These Meals Healthier

⭐ How would you make the following meals healthier? Use the guidelines of MyPlate or Healthy Eating Plate on pages 26 and 27 to help. Include more vegetables, whole grains, legumes, fruits, and dairy... and use your imagination!

| Meal 1 | Meal 2 | Meal 3 | Meal 4 | Meal 5 |
|---|---|---|---|---|
| Fried chicken<br><br>White rice<br><br>Salad with lettuce and cucumbers<br><br>Whole milk | Hamburger on white bun<br><br>French fries<br><br>Milk shake | Pasta<br><br>Tomato sauce<br><br>Garlic bread with butter<br><br>Soda | Instant Ramen<br><br>Chips<br><br>Juice | Stir-fry with beef and white rice |
|  |  |  |  |  |

# Food Journal

## ★ Are you aware of how you eat?

Keep a food journal for a day. Write down the types of foods and amounts. Describe the circumstances including people, time, place, and environment. Note your mood and energy after and throughout the day.

| Date | What I Ate | With Who, When, Where | How I Felt |
|---|---|---|---|
| Breakfast | | | |
| Lunch | | | |
| Dinner | | | |
| Snacks | | | |

» How did the circumstances affect what and how you ate?

» Do you notice a relationship between how you felt and how you ate?

30

# CHOOSING WHOLE FOODS

# Food Processing

■ **The more a food is processed, the fewer health benefits it tends to have.**

Food processing is when a whole food is changed from its original form. It can include anything ranging from simple grinding of wheat to make flour to using industrial machines to make convenience foods.

The best foods for health are **whole foods,** which are unprocessed or just barely processed. They don't usually come with an ingredient list or only one ingredient is listed on the package.

**Minimally-processed foods** are foods we buy ready to use or are processed to last longer or to change the taste. In many cases, these can be healthy choices.

**Ultra-processed foods** are highly processed in factories using industrial equipment and techniques and tend to have very long ingredient lists. They are engineered to make you want to eat more. Flavored potato chips may be one example.

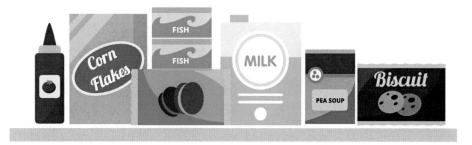

★ *Here are tips for choosing healthier packaged and processed foods:*

» Choose foods made from ingredients that you can picture in their original state or growing in nature. If you see something you can't pronounce, look out.

» Don't be fooled by big health claims on a package. Health claims such as "low-fat" can distract you from something less healthy such as high sugar or sodium.

» Avoid foods with sugar listed in the first three ingredients. Look out for hidden added sugars.

» Look for 100% whole grain foods; find this label or the word "whole" in the first ingredient (whole oats, whole wheat, whole corn).

---

**THINK ABOUT IT** ▶

How is food processing helpful? How can it be harmful?

What processed foods do you often eat? What processed foods would you like to eat less of or avoid?

---

*[continues on next page...]*

# Food Processing (CONTINUED)

**TRY IT!** Foods can range between whole foods and ultra-processed foods. Draw a line from the food to where you think it falls on the processing spectrum. In the last section, add your own items and draw a line to where you think they fall on the spectrum.

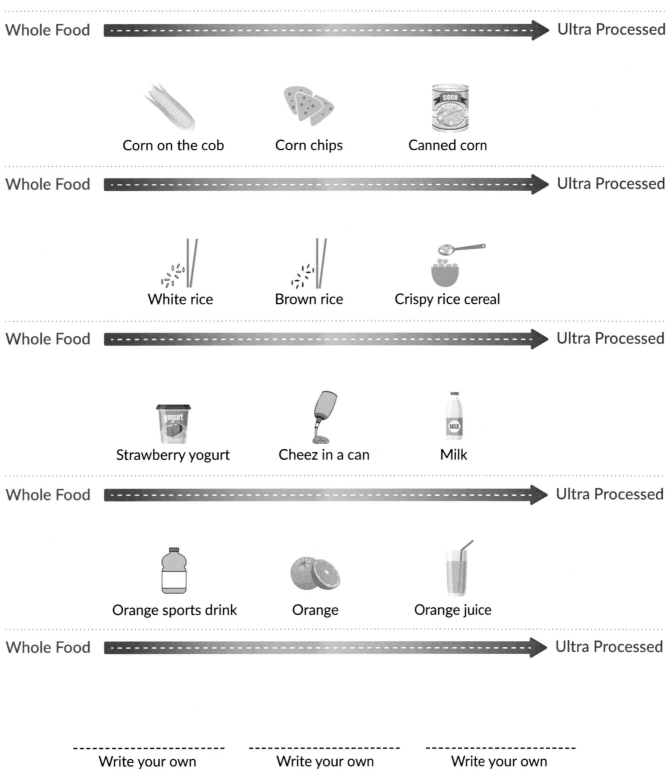

Whole Food ——————————————→ Ultra Processed

Corn on the cob    Corn chips    Canned corn

Whole Food ——————————————→ Ultra Processed

White rice    Brown rice    Crispy rice cereal

Whole Food ——————————————→ Ultra Processed

Strawberry yogurt    Cheez in a can    Milk

Whole Food ——————————————→ Ultra Processed

Orange sports drink    Orange    Orange juice

Whole Food ——————————————→ Ultra Processed

———————————    ———————————    ———————————
Write your own    Write your own    Write your own

# Building Your Fire

★ Some foods fuel our body for a long time, some for a little, and not very long at all. What foods can we eat to make our bodies as strong and healthy as possible? One way we can think about eating is that we are using food to build a fire in our bodies.

Eating **whole foods** is like building a fire with logs. Your fire will burn bright and strong and last a long time.

Some **minimally-processed foods** also can help build a good fire especially if you eat them along with whole foods.

Eating **ultra-processed foods** are like building a fire with sticks or paper. They might burn for a minute but your fire will not last very long, and it will not give your body what it needs to be at its best.

In the logs, write the name of the foods that you want in your body to build a good roaring fire.

# My Family's Rainbow

★ Fill in the chart with the fruits and vegetables you and your family eat the most. What colors are missing?

| ★ Green Foods | ★ Red Foods |
|---|---|
| | |
| ★ Yellow/Orange Foods | ★ Blue/Purple Foods |
| | |
| ★ White Foods | ★ Others |
| | |

# Eat the Rainbow!

★ **Which color do you eat the most? Eating a variety helps your body stay healthy.**

★ *Green Foods*

» Lower your chance of getting cancer

» Keep your eyes healthy

» Keep your bones & teeth strong

**TRY IT!**

spinach            kale
celery             artichokes
green beans        honeydew
broccoli           green grapes
cabbage            green apples
bok choy           limes
cucumbers          avocados
asparagus

★ *Yellow & Orange Foods*

» Keep your heart healthy

» Keep your eyes healthy

» Lower your chance of getting cancer

» Keep you from catching colds

**TRY IT!**

carrots            cantaloupe
sweet potatoes     tangerines
yellow peppers     mangoes
pumpkins           oranges
pineapple          lemons
papayas            peaches

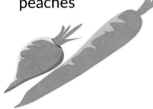

★ *Red Foods*

» Keep your heart healthy

» Keep your bladder healthy

» Keep your memory strong

» Lower your chance of getting cancer

**TRY IT!**

tomatoes           watermelon
red peppers        red onion
red cabbage        red apples
strawberries       beets
cherries

★ *Blue & Purple Foods*

» Stay healthy when you get old

» Keep your memory strong

» Keep your bladder healthy

» Lower your chance of getting cancer

**TRY IT!**

eggplant           blueberries
purple cabbage     blackberries
raisins            purple grapes

★ *White Foods*

» Keep your heart healthy

» Have good cholesterol levels

» Lower your chance of getting cancer

**TRY IT!**

onion              ginger
green onion        garlic
cauliflower        jicama
chives             fennel
mushrooms

# Make Half Your Grains Whole

## ★ Why choose whole grains?

Whole grains are usually darker in color and stronger in flavor than refined grains and flours. Eating whole grains has been shown to lower the risk for diabetes, heart disease, high cholesterol, and high blood pressure.

A whole grain contains the germ, endosperm and bran, while a refined or processed grain only contains the endosperm. The germ and bran are the most nutrient rich parts of the grain, and the highest in fiber. Check the ingredient list to make sure you're getting a truly whole grain product: the first ingredient should be something like "whole wheat" and not just "wheat."

Sometimes whole grains can be identified with this stamp:

---

| REFINED GRAIN FOODS (endosperm only) | WHOLE GRAINS (bran + endosperm + germ) | |
|---|---|---|
| » White pasta | » Oats | » Farro |
| » White bread | » Brown rice | » Spelt |
| » Most cakes, cookies, and pastries | » Whole wheat | » Quinoa |
| | » Barley | » Millet |
| | » Buckwheat | » Teff |

---

**Bran: protects the seed**

- » Fiber
- » B vitamins
- » Minerals

**Endosperm: energy for the seed**

- » Carbohydrates
- » Some protein
- » Some B vitamins

**Germ: nourishment for the seed**

- » B vitamins
- » Vitamin E
- » Minerals
- » Phytochemicals

## DID YOU KNOW?

A diet rich in fiber, as found in whole grains and beans, helps your digestion and keeps you full for longer. Make sure to get 3 servings of whole grains and 4½ cups of fruits and veggies each day for the recommended amount of fiber.

# Grain Game

## ★ Can you identify different whole grains?

Grains have been an important source of energy for thousands of years. Whole or unrefined grains that contain all parts of the seed provide important nutrients such as fiber, minerals, healthy fats, disease-fighting antioxidants, and several are a good source of complete protein. Can you match the grain with its description? Write the number next to the definition.

___ **AMARANTH**, an ancient grain that was cultivated in South America since about 8000 years ago. Amaranth has a peppery taste with a pleasantly sweet, grassy aroma. It's tiny grains can be prepared in porridge or polenta style recipes. It can also be popped like popcorn!

___ **BARLEY** is one of the world's earliest grains from Ancient China to Europe and Africa. It was even a food for gladiators (who mostly ate a vegetarian diet!). To be sure you are getting the best nutrition, look for barley labeled as whole, hulled, or hull-less. You might have had barley in soup but it makes a good substitute for rice in many dishes.

___ **BROWN RICE** is a whole grain while white rice is not. Brown rice contains double the nutrition as refined white rice. Other whole grain rice can be black, purple, or red. Wild rice is not actually rice but is also very nutritious and flavorful.

___ **BUCKWHEAT** is not a type of wheat—in fact it's not technically a grain at all but is used just like one! Buckwheat has a strong flavor. Buckwheat flour is used for traditional noodles like Japanese soba while cracked buckwheat makes a good hot porridge.

___ **BULGUR WHEAT** is produced when whole wheat kernels are cleaned, boiled, dried, and grounded. It needs to be boiled for only about 10 minutes to be ready to eat, making it great for side dishes, pilafs, or salads. Middle Eastern tabbouleh is a famous salad prepared with bulgur.

___ **CORN** is more than just sweet corn that we enjoy with butter and salt. Popcorn is a type of flint corn grown by Indigenous Americans. It's a delicious whole grain snack. Dried field corn kernels, also called hominy, can be used in soups or side dishes. Masa, a ground hominy dough, is used to make corn tortillas. Ground hominy corn is also used to make porridges like grits and polenta.

___ **MILLET** is mentioned in Ancient Greek and Ancient Roman texts and was common in Medieval Europe. It can be used to make sweet or savory porridges, baked goods and flat breads in Indian and Ethiopian cuisine.

___ **OATS** have been around since the earliest humans! Whether they are rolled or steel cut, oats are almost always in their whole grain form. They are good breakfast foods because oats keep you full longer. Oats can also be used in savory dishes like jook/congee or risotto.

### ■ Cooking Tip

Whole grain kernels can be cooked like rice but may require differing amounts of water or cooking time. Most can be used as a substitute when rice is called for in sweet or savory recipes. Or if you are still getting used to eating whole grains, mix some into your white rice to improve its nourishment.

*[continues on next page...]*

# Grain Game (CONTINUED)

__ **QUINOA** is not exactly a grain, but these tiny kernels can be eaten like one. In fact, it is actually related to spinach! It was sacred to the Ancient Mayans who considered it "the mother of all grains." Quinoa cooks quickly and is delicious in warm and cold grain salads and as a side dish.

__ **WHEAT BERRIES** are the individual wheat kernels that can be cooked like rice to be enjoyed as a side dish. Red wheat berries are produced from a modern wheat plant. Spelt and farro are a type of wheat berry are more similar to what was first grown by humans over 10,000 years ago!

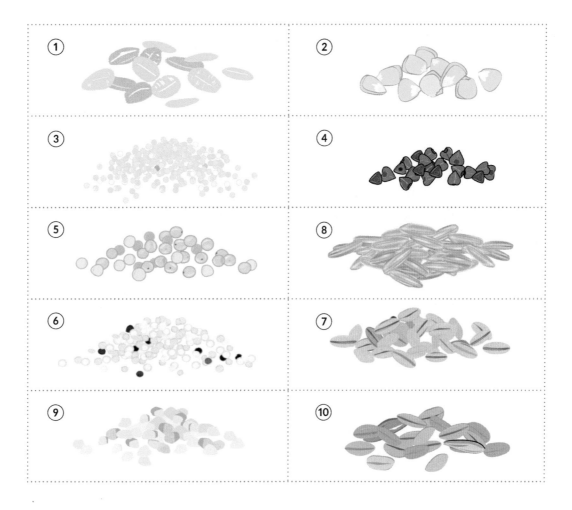

Answers: 1. Oats, 2. Corn, 3. Amaranth, 4. Buckwheat, 5. Millet, 6. Quinoa, 7. Wheat berries, 8. Brown rice, 9. Bulgur wheat, 10. Barley.

# Bean Game

## ★ What beans do you know?

Beans contain nutrients—especially protein and fiber—that we need to heal our bodies, prevent heart disease and cancer, support digestion, and build new muscle, bone, hair, teeth and blood. They have been an important part of cuisines around the world for thousands of years. Can you match the bean with its description? Write the number next to the definition.

\_\_ **SOY BEANS** originated from Asia and commonly used to make many delicious foods and drinks like soy milk, tofu, tempeh, soybean oil, and many vegetarian options. Have you ever had edamame? They cook quickly and have a sweet, buttery flavor..

\_\_ **CHICKPEAS (or GARBANZO BEANS)** have a nutty buttery flavor and creamy texture. They are very common in middle eastern, Mediterranean, Indian, Spanish and French cooking, but are also found in many cuisines around the world. They can be ground up or pureed to make falafel and hummus. Cooked whole chickpeas are great in salads and stews.

\_\_ **BLACK BEANS** are sweet-tasting with a soft texture. They are popular in Central American, South American, and Caribbean cuisine. Black beans and rice is a common dish that goes by names such as Congrí, Moros y Christianos, and Casamiento in Spanish-speaking countries.

\_\_ **SPLIT PEAS** are dried field peas (green peas are a type of young field pea). Yellow or green split peas are commonly used to make soups around the world—Green Split Pea (North America & Europe), Dal (India), and Tamaraqt (Morocco). In fact, the Greeks and Romans were making split pea soup since at least 500 B.C.

\_\_ **KIDNEY BEANS** have a firm texture, and are a great addition to salads. They also hold up well in soups and stews like American chili, or other dishes that cook for a long time. Light red kidney beans are popular in the Caribbean region, Portugal, and Spain.

\_\_ **SMALL RED BEANS** have a more delicate flavor and softer texture compared to kidney beans. Small red beans are particularly popular in the Caribbean region, where they traditionally are eaten with rice. Small red beans are also used to make Louisiana Red Beans & Rice.

\_\_ **LENTILS** come in a wide variety of colors, sizes and textures. Some varieties are red, brown, blue-green, yellow, or black. The term lentil comes from the word for lens, which describes the shape of these legumes. Lentils are an ancient food-Archaeologists found evidence of lentils in Greek ruins from 11,000 B.C!

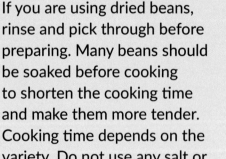

## ■ Cooking Tip

If you are using dried beans, rinse and pick through before preparing. Many beans should be soaked before cooking to shorten the cooking time and make them more tender. Cooking time depends on the variety. Do not use any salt or acidic ingredients while cooking. Canned beans can be rinsed to reduce the sodium content.

*[continues on next page...]*

# Bean Game (CONTINUED)

__ **BLACK-EYED PEAS** have an earthy, nutty taste. They originated in West Africa and were introduced to the Americas by enslaved people. Hoppin' John is a soul food tradition that is meant to bring good luck for the New Year. Middle Eastern, Asian, Indian, Caribbean, South American, and European cultures also use black-eyed peas.

__ **PINTO BEANS** got their name from the Spanish word for "speckled," but they lose their spotted appearance when cooked. Pinto beans are the most widely produced bean in the U.S. and are used to make Mexican refried beans.

__ **NAVY BEANS** have a mild, delicate flavor. These are the beans used in Boston Baked Beans. These white beans were named Navy Beans because they were fed to sailors in the U.S. Navy in the 1800's.

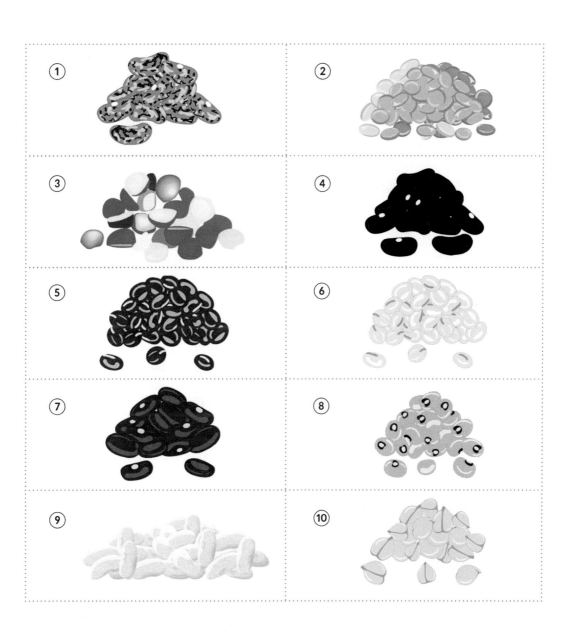

Answers: 1. Pinto beans, 2. Lentils, 3. Split peas, 4. Black beans, 5. Small red beans, 6. Soy beans, 7. Kidney beans, 8. Black-eyed peas, 9. Navy beans, 10. Chickpeas.

# Garden Sort

★ Does it grow on a tree? *Circle it.*

★ Does it grow underground? *Put an X on it.*

★ Does it grow on a bush? *Put a box around it.*

★ Does it grow on a vine? *Put a star next to it.*

★ What's left? How does it grow?

# Plant Parts We Eat

★ Think of your favorite plant foods. Which parts of the plant do they come from? Try and fill in the boxes with foods from each part.

**Fruit**

**Flowers**

**Seeds**

**Leaves**

**Stems**

**Roots**

★ *We even eat the bark of some trees! Can you name the common brown spice that comes from tree bark? Hint: it is used in desserts like apple pie.*

# Eating In-Season

## ★ What's growing near you now?

Certain fruits and vegetables grow at certain times of the year. Fresh fruits and vegetables eaten while in-season taste better and provide more nutritional benefits. For example, a strawberry eaten in the summer will be sweeter and will contain more vitamin C than a strawberry eaten in December. The chart below outlines what fruits and vegetables you might see in North America at your local food pantry and farmers' market each season.

### Available All Year
- » Beets
- » Cabbage
- » Carrots
- » Cauliflower
- » Mushrooms
- » Onions
- » Oranges
- » Potatoes
- » Spinach

### Summer
- » Berries
- » Corn
- » Eggplant
- » Grapes
- » Pears
- » Tomatoes
- » Watermelon
- » Zucchini
- » Peaches, plums, apricots, cherries

### Fall
- » Apples
- » Peppers
- » Sweet potatoes
- » Winter squash

### Winter-Spring
- » Asparagus
- » Hard squashes
- » Sweet potatoes
- » Turnips and broccoli

44

# Fuel Your Brain

Did you know that what you eat affects your brain? Here are some tips on fueling your brain to the max.

## ★ How can eating whole foods help your brain?

When we don't eat enough of the nutrients found in whole foods, our mood, energy and thinking could be affected. Fuel yourself during the day with foods that will help you stay focused and energetic.

### ★ *Breakfast*

Maintaining energy and concentration is an important part of a healthy lifestyle. Breakfast is the first place to start. A good breakfast may help you keep a steady energy and mood later in the day. Choose to eat a healthy, balanced breakfast over sugar and caffeine. **Choose to eat a healthy, balanced breakfast over sugar and caffeine.**

| Instead of... | Try... |
| --- | --- |
| sugary cereal | oats or shredded wheat |
| coffee | green tea |
| juice | whole fruit or diluted juice |
| pastries, danishes, or donuts | whole wheat toast w/cream cheese or peanut butter |

### ★ *Lunch*

What do you eat for lunch? Do you bring it from home or get it at school? How do you feel before lunch—hungry or famished? How do you feel after lunch—energized or sleepy? **Choose to eat a healthy, balanced lunch (and a mid-morning snack).**

| Instead of... | Try... |
| --- | --- |
| potato chips | almonds or sunflower seeds |
| soda | water or milk |
| candy | fruit |
| pizza or fast food | veggie wrap or turkey sandwich |

### ▮ Eggs...

» are great for a quick breakfast, lunch or snack. They can help you steady your mood and energy. A hardboiled egg or a quick scramble on the stove or in the microwave are easy options.

# Rethink Your Drink

⭐ **How much sugar is in your favorite drink? Use the nutrition facts to find out.**

» Use the nutrition facts to find out.
» Check the number of servings per container. Will you drink more than one?
» For each serving, do the math: grams of sugar ÷ 4 = teaspoons of sugar
  For example: 40g sugar ÷ 4 = 10 teaspoons sugar

**TRY IT!** Now do the math on these other soft drinks. How many teaspoons of sugar in each serving? In each bottle or can?

**ORANGE SODA**
## Nutrition Facts
Serving Size 8 oz.
Servings per Container 2

| Amount per Serving | |
| --- | --- |
| Calories 168  Calories from Fat 0 | |
| Total Fat 0g | |
| Saturated Fat 0g | |
| Trans Fat 0g | |
| Cholesterol 0mg | |
| Sodium 50mg | |
| Total Carbohydrate 42g | |
| Dietary Fiber 0g | |
| Sugars 42g | |
| Protein 0g | |
| Vitamin D 0%  Calcium 0% | |
| Potassium 0%  Iron 0% | |

**CHOCOLATE MILK**
## Nutrition Facts
Serving Size 8 oz.
Servings per Container 1

| Amount per Serving | |
| --- | --- |
| Calories 193  Calories from Fat 81 | |
| Total Fat 9g | |
| Saturated Fat 5g | |
| Trans Fat 0g | |
| Cholesterol 35mg | |
| Sodium 125mg | |
| Total Carbohydrate 20g | |
| Dietary Fiber 0g | |
| Sugars 20g | |
| Protein 8g | |
| Vitamin D 15%  Calcium 25% | |
| Potassium 10%  Iron 0% | |

**SWEET TEA**
## Nutrition Facts
Serving Size 8 oz.
Servings per Container 3

| Amount per Serving | |
| --- | --- |
| Calories 144  Calories from Fat 0 | |
| Total Fat 0g | |
| Saturated Fat 0g | |
| Trans Fat 0g | |
| Cholesterol 0mg | |
| Sodium 50mg | |
| Total Carbohydrate 36g | |
| Dietary Fiber 0g | |
| Sugars 36g | |
| Protein 0g | |
| Vitamin D 0%  Calcium 0% | |
| Potassium 0%  Iron 0% | |

**COLA**
## Nutrition Facts
Serving Size 1 can (12 fl. oz.)
Servings per Container 1

| Amount per Serving | |
| --- | --- |
| Calories 150  Calories from Fat 0 | |
| Total Fat 0g | |
| Saturated Fat 0g | |
| Trans Fat 0g | |
| Cholesterol 0mg | |
| Sodium 50mg | |
| Total Carbohydrate 40g | |
| Dietary Fiber 0g | |
| Sugars 40g | |
| Protein 0g | |
| Vitamin A 0%  Vitamin C 0% | |
| Iron 0%  Iron 0%  Calcium 0% | |

# Rethink Your Drink (CONTINUED)

## ★ Drink Water Instead!

» Add lemon to your water for extra flavor. Or try the recipe below.

» Try drinking hot, cold, and room temperature water to see what you like best.

» Have a glass of water on the table at every meal, and nearby when working.

» Drink a glass in the morning after waking up.

» Drink water instead of snacking.

» Drink water when you eat out. It's free!

» Note that in many places, tap water must meet many more standards than bottled water! Bottled water also sits in plastic. This may be harmful to human health and the Earth. Consider saving money and drinking local tap water from a reusable glass or metal bottle.

### ★ *Flavored Water Recipe*

Fill a pitcher with cool water.

Add ½ cup thinly sliced cucumber and ½ cup fresh mint leaves. Chill in refrigerator. Enjoy!

Try different combinations of flavors:

» Thin slices: lemon, lime, orange, grapefruit, cucumber, apple, berries, melon, pineapple, fresh ginger

» Fresh whole leaves or sprigs: mint, basil, rosemary, parsley

# Don't Call Me Sugar!

★ There are many names for the sugar added to food. Can you find the ones hidden here?

BARLEY MALT

BROWN SUGAR

CANE JUICE

CORN SYRUP

DEXTRIN

DEXTROSE

FRUCTOSE

GLUCOSE

HONEY

LACTOSE

MALTOSE

MAPLE SYRUP

MOLASSES

SWEETENER

```
H  O  N  E  Y  F  E  M  A  T  R  A  P  S  A
M  E  N  U  K  S  W  E  E  T  E  N  E  R  N
T  A  N  I  R  A  H  C  C  A  S  E  H  F  A
U  R  R  S  O  R  B  I  T  O  L  O  M  R  Y
R  N  I  R  T  X  E  D  C  R  A  C  A  U  W
G  A  S  M  M  E  E  O  J  I  S  L  P  C  T
L  I  G  R  B  A  R  L  E  Y  M  A  L  T  E
U  E  T  U  Y  N  M  X  Q  O  E  C  E  O  E
C  S  E  S  S  A  L  O  M  S  E  T  S  S  W
O  U  L  Y  L  N  K  L  O  T  L  O  Y  E  S
S  O  R  T  H  Y  W  R  E  T  C  S  R  B  A
E  U  O  D  H  T  T  O  O  N  L  E  U  H  R
P  S  T  P  G  X  V  Z  R  T  U  P  P  F  T
E  T  C  M  E  W  B  C  A  B  D  M  G  A  U
S  T  R  D  B  C  A  N  E  J  U  I  C  E  N
```

**BONUS** ▶ Can you find these artificial sweeteners too?
These are chemicals with few or no calories.

ASPARTAME      NUTRASWEET      SACCHARIN      SORBITOL

48

# GROCERY SHOPPING

# Healthy Swaps

★ True or False: Healthy foods always cost more money than unhealthy foods? Choosing healthier foods doesn't necessarily mean spending more money.

| Instead of... | Try... |
| --- | --- |
| flour tortillas<br>$0.20 each | corn tortillas<br>$0.09 each |
| potato chips<br>$0.36/oz | popcorn<br>$0.10/oz |
| sugary cereal<br>$0.28/oz | oatmeal<br>$0.16/oz |
| white bread<br>$0.08/oz | whole wheat bread<br>$0.08/oz |
| white rice<br>$0.08/oz | brown rice<br>$0.08/oz |
| white pasta<br>$0.13/oz | whole wheat pasta<br>$0.07/oz |

*Price comparison research done in Huntington Beach CA, 2021. Prices in your area may differ.*

# Nutrition Words to Know

★ **Do you know these words from the nutrition facts label? Try to match each to its definition.**

| | |
|---|---|
| Different colored fruits and vegetables have different___. Our bodies need these in small amounts to fight infections and prevent diseases. | fat |
| ____ come from bread, rice, and many other foods. Your body uses them for energy. | carbohydrates |
| Foods like butter and oil have a lot of ___. A little is good for you, but too much is not. | calories |
| ___ can make foods taste salty. Too much is not healthy. | fiber |
| The number of ___ in a food is how much energy the food can give your body. | sodium |
| ___ helps your digestion and keeps you full and energized longer. | sugars |
| ___ make food sweet and give your body quick energy. | protein |
| Your muscles are made up of ___. You can get it from many animal foods, like meat. You can also get it from plant foods like nuts and tofu. | vitamins and minerals |

Here are some other nutrition words you may have heard:

» **Gluten** is found in certain grains, like wheat. Some people cannot eat it.

» **Vegetarians** do not eat meat.

» **Vegans** do not eat any animal products at all, including milk or eggs.

» **Organic** foods have been grown or produced without pesticides or harmful chemicals.

 **TRY IT!** Next time you look at a food package, try to find words you don't know. How can you discover what they mean?

# Food Labels—Nutrition Facts

★ **What do you look for on a nutrition label? Choose one or two items to concentrate on at a time.**

**❶** Check the Serving Size and Servings per Container. Remember the Nutrition Facts label is for one serving. Your package might have more than one serving. If you are eating two servings, then you need to double everything on the labels.

**❷** Calories tells you how much energy you get from eating one serving of this food. Fat-free does not mean calories-free. Items that are fat-free, low-fat, or reduced-fat might have the same amount of calories as the full fat version.

**❸** The total fat on the label might include monounsaturated and polyunsaturated fats, which are "good fats" that can help lower blood cholesterol. "Zero Trans Fat" foods don't always mean the food is trans-fat-free. The law allows a small amount of trans fat per serving in foods. Read the ingredient list and look for "partially hydrogenated oils" to see if the food has trans fat. Consume foods low in added sugars, saturated fats, and sodium. Cut back on foods higher in these nutrients.

**❹** Getting enough dietary fiber, vitamins, and minerals can improve your overall health and help reduce the risk of some diseases. Choose foods with higher % Daily Value for these nutrients. Fiber also promotes healthy bowel function.

**❺** The footnote states that the % Daily Value on the nutrition label is based on a 2,000-calorie-diet. This is a recommendation. The amount that each person needs depends on their caloric needs. It also breaks down the nutrient needs for a 2,500 calorie eating pattern.

**❻** % Daily Value on the nutrition labels helps you determine if a serving of that food is high or low in those nutrients. The guide is to choose products that are 5% Daily Value or less for things you want to limit like saturated fat, and sodium. Look for 20% Daily Value or more for things you want to eat more of.

# Food Labels—Nutrition Facts (CONTINUED)

**1 Start here**

**2 Check calories**

**3 Limit these nutrients**

**4 Get enough of these nutrients**

**5 Footnote**

## Nutrition Facts

**2 servings per container**
**Serving Size 1 cup**

**Amount Per Serving**

**Calories 250**

| | % Daily Value |
|---|---|
| **Total Fat** 12g | 18% |
| Saturated Fat 3g | 15% |
| Trans Fat 3g | |
| **Cholesterol** 30mg | 10% |
| **Sodium** 470mg | 20% |
| **Total Carbohydrate** 31g | 10% |
| Dietary Fiber | 0% |
| Total Sugars 5g | |
| Includes 2g Added Sugars | |
| **Protein** 5g | |
| Vitamin D | 4% |
| Calcium | 2% |
| Iron | 20% |
| Potassium | 4% |

\* The % Daily Value (DV) tells you how much a nutrient in a serving contributes to a daily diet. 2,000 calories a day is used for general nutrition advice

**6 Quick guide to % DV**

5% or less is Low

20% or more is High

© Copyright 2018-2022 Leah's Pantry Food Smarts Kids Workbook

# Food Label Scavenger Hunt

★ **How do you choose between two products to find the healthier option?**

Compare the two labels on the next page or from two similar products.

★ *Which food label has...*

| | Label A | Label B |
|---|---|---|
| 1.   More **calories** per serving | Label A | Label B |
| 2.   More **sugar** per serving | Label A | Label B |
| 3.   Less **sodium** per serving | Label A | Label B |
| 4.   More **saturated fat** per serving | Label A | Label B |
| 5.   More **fiber** per serving | Label A | Label B |
| 6.   More **calories** from fat | Label A | Label B |
| 7.   More **protein** per serving | Label A | Label B |
| 8.   More **total fat** per serving | Label A | Label B |
| 9.   More **calcium** per serving | Label A | Label B |
| 10.  Which would you choose? Why? | Label A | Label B |

# Food Label Scavenger Hunt (CONTINUED)

★ **Can you guess what food these labels come from?**

## Label A

### Nutrition Facts

8 Servings per Container

Serving Size ............ 1 bar

**Amount Per Serving**

## Calories 120

| | % Daily Value* |
|---|---|
| **Total Fat** 3g | 5% |
| Saturated Fat 1g | 3% |
| *Trans* Fat 0g | |
| **Cholesterol** 0mg | 0% |
| **Sodium** 110mg | 5% |
| **Total Carbohydrate** 24g | 8% |
| Dietary Fiber 3g | 10% |
| Total Sugars 11g | |
| Includes 9g Added Sugars | |
| **Protein** 2g | |
| Vitamin D 0mcg | 0% |
| Calcium 48mcg | 4% |
| Iron 3mg | 11% |
| Potassium 329mg | 7% |

* The % Daily Value (DV) tells you how much a nutrient in a serving of food contributes to a daily diet. 2,000 calories a day is used for general nutrition advice.

**Ingredients:** whole grain oats, enriched flour (wheat flour, niacin, reduced iron, thiamin mononitrate, riboflavin, folic acid), whole wheat flour, vegetable oil (high oleic soybean and/or canola oil), soluble corn fiber, sugar, dextrose, fructose, calcium carbonate, whey, wheat bran, cellulose, potassium bicarbonate, natural and artificial flavor, mono- and diglycerides, soy lecithin, wheat gluten, niacinimide, vitamin A palmitate, carrageenan, zinc oxide, guar gum, pyridoxine hydrochloride, thiamin hydrochloride; filling: invert sugar, corn syrup, glycerin, apple puree concentrate, sugar, blueberry puree concentrate, natural and artificial flavors, raspberry puree concentrate, modified cornstarch, sodium alginate, citric acid, malic acid, methylcellulose, dicalcium phosphate, red 40, blue 1

## Label B

### Nutrition Facts

12 Servings per Container

Serving Size ............ 1 bar

**Amount Per Serving**

## Calories 144

| | % Daily Value* |
|---|---|
| **Total Fat** 5g | 6% |
| Saturated Fat 0g | 2% |
| *Trans* Fat 0g | |
| **Cholesterol** 0mg | 0% |
| **Sodium** 83mg | 3% |
| **Total Carbohydrate** 23g | 7% |
| Dietary Fiber 2g | 8% |
| Total Sugars 8g | |
| Includes 6g Added Sugars | |
| **Protein** 3g | |
| Vitamin D 0mcg | 0% |
| Calcium 18mcg | 1% |
| Iron 1mg | 5% |
| Potassium 97mg | 2% |

* The % Daily Value (DV) tells you how much a nutrient in a serving of food contributes to a daily diet. 2,000 calories a day is used for general nutrition advice.

**Ingredients:** whole grain oats, almonds, raisins, honey, canola oil, cinnamon, salt

*Nutrition Labels, (2016 Dietary Guidelines)*

# Anatomy of a Grocery Store

★ How does the layout of your grocery store shape your choices? Draw a diagram that shows what you would find in each part of the store.

# Outsmarting the Grocery Store

★ **Now discuss your store map with classmates.**

★ *Do you know?*

» Where are the healthiest foods located?

» Are products displayed at the ends of aisles always on sale?

» Is there usually a difference in price between name brand and generic products? What about quality?

» Why are candy and magazines always near the register?

» Where are the most expensive products located on the shelves? What about cereals marketed to kids?

» When should you put refrigerated and frozen foods in your basket? Why?

★ *A few tips:*

» **Unit prices** allow you to compare the price of two packages that may contain a different amount of food.

» **Larger packages** often have lower unit prices; however, be sure to consider whether you'll be able to eat the entire amount before it goes bad. Find stores that carry bulk foods.

» **Generic products** are often identical to name brand products in everything but price.

» Often, foods sold from the **bulk bin** are less expensive by weight than foods sold in packages.

**THINK ABOUT IT**

Which foods are furthest from the front door? Why do you think so?

Why do you think canned and boxed foods are placed in the middle aisles?

# Creating a Meal Plan & Grocery List

★ Think of a meal you would like to make. (Find recipes on your own or choose from EatFresh.org) Then make a plan.

★ *How do I do it?*

**1** Using your recipes, make a grocery list that includes all of the ingredients for each recipe. Make sure to check your kitchen for main ingredients such as olive oil, salt, and pepper. You probably don't need to buy everything.

**2** Sort your grocery list according to type of food: produce, meat, dairy and dry goods. Try to guess how much of each thing you need to buy.

**3** Grocery shop! Save the receipt to help create a budget for the future.

**4** Review your receipt afterwards. Do you see anything surprising?

★ *Meal Plan & Grocery List*

| Meals | Grocery list |
|---|---|
|  | Produce |
|  | Meat |
|  | Dairy |
|  | Dry, Canned, or Boxed |

58

# Food Marketing

★ **Where have you noticed these strategies used by companies to get you to buy their product? Have you ever been influenced by them?**

» **Ads everywhere:** Ads are put in many places, especially on the internet, social media and video streaming platforms, to constantly remind us about the food product. The product can also be marketed along with a new movie or video game

» **Exaggerated images:** The food looks better than real life. Extreme closeups trigger our senses of taste and smell, making us crave that food.

» **Heartwarming:** Kids and families in the ad look perfect and happy, making it seem the food brings them together.

» **Claims about the taste or popularity:** The food's deliciousness or popularity is exaggerated by unsupported claims.

» **Using celebrities, influencers or cartoon characters**: Famous faces make us feel personally connected to the product.

» **"Health Halo"/"Green Washing":** The product seems healthy, more natural, or better for the environment, especially with words like "all natural" or certain colors and images.

» **Overdoing it:** You may feel encouraged to eat a lot of the product when you see people who can't stop enjoying it.

» **Coupons, Contests, Games or Giveaways:** Prizes and fun contests make you want to buy one brand instead of another.

» **Donations, Sponsorships, and Charities:** Messages of doing good in the world encourage you to buy it.

» **Many Points of Sale:** The product is sold everywhere including in hospitals and schools.

» **Shelf Position:** Companies pay fees to grocery stories so products can be easy to spot on the shelves.

# STAYING HEALTHY

# Make Moving Fun!

★ **What are your favorite ways to move? Kids need 60 minutes of exercise daily. How do you get your 60 minutes?**

» Limit "Screen" Time (mobile devices, computer, TV, video games). More hours of screen time per week is directly connected to less movement and poorer health.

» Physical activity builds strength and endurance. It can also improve mood, sleep, energy, and concentration!

» If you have a tough time getting motivated, look for ways to be active with others—go for walks, dance with a buddy, or add physical games to a family party. Anything that involves movement is better than sitting and watching a screen.

*"Nothing happens until something moves."*
*- Albert Einstein*

**THINK ABOUT IT**

Do you get enough exercise every week? Does your family?

What are some ways to move more during your day?

★ *A few tips for getting exercise without a gym*

» Jump rope

» Jumping jacks

» Dance parties

» Wrestling

» Housework

» Stairs instead of the elevator

» Yoga or stretching

» Hula Hoop

 **TRY IT!** What is one fun movement activity you will try this week?

62

# Healthy Changes

★ **What advice would you give to these kids?**

❶ Jesse hates to get up in the morning! She would rather sleep in than eat breakfast. But by the time she gets to school, she feels hungry and tired. She often falls asleep in class. She eats mostly from the school cafeteria, but usually chooses foods like apples, chocolate milk, and french fries. After school, she often snacks on soda, cookies, and candy. Her mom comes home late but tries to cook a healthy dinner when she can.

❷ Tony is an athlete who has practice almost every day after school. He needs to eat a lot! He eats cereal in the morning, lunch in the cafeteria and a fast food meal every day before practice. His family likes to eat big dinners like homemade beef tacos with rice and beans. He's really active, and is concerned about staying strong, fast and having enough energy to play.

❸ Jill doesn't eat regular meals. If she's up on time, she eats breakfast but often skips lunch because she doesn't like the food in the cafeteria. She likes to drink iced mochas and eats mostly fruit, cheese, veggies, and bread. Some nights she has to make her own dinner. She often stays up late studying and will snack around 11pm.

★ *If you were in their shoes*

» What changes would you make?

» What help and support might you need?

» What SMART goal would you create?

# Eating Out and Staying Healthy

★ **Do you make different food choices when eat out? It's easy to over do it when eating out.**

» Rethink Your Drink: choose water over sugar-sweetened choices.

» Ask for sauces and dressings on the side. Dip instead of pour!

» Choose salsa and mustard over mayo and oil.

» Avoid dishes with these words: au gratin, breaded, buttered, cheesy, creamy, gravy, scalloped, fried, battered.

» Choose dishes with these words: baked, broiled, poached, grilled, roasted, steamed.

» Split entrees with your friend.

» Consider serving sizes carefully. Can your craving for french fries be satisfied by a small instead of a large order?

» If the portions are large, set aside food to take home before you dig in.

» Bring the food home and add a side of raw veggies or fruit to complete the meal.

» Drive past the drive-thru; it's difficult to find healthy fast food on the run!

**TRY IT!** Another way to approach healthy eating when you eat out is to think about your diet for the whole day. Write down a favorite restaurant meal. Use MyPlate or My Healthy Eating Plate (pages 26 and 27) to consider how you can balance out the day. List what you would choose for your other meals and snacks for the day.

★ **Favorite Restaurant Meal**

★ **Other Meals and Snacks**

# Sleep Your Way to Health

★ **Do you get enough rest? Sleep is important for your body.**

Word bank:

hours

liver

minutes

more

humans

memories

sleep

blood

hormones

clean

## ACROSS

1. You may eat _____ when you're tired.

2. Most adults need at least 7–9 _____ of sleep per night, even seniors. Children need more.

3. Your brain can _____ itself during sleep by getting rid of waste.

6. Sleep helps the brain form _____.

7. During deep sleep, your _____ pressure drops. Breathing slows and blood flow moves to the muscles.

8. The Challenger shuttle disaster and Chernobyl nuclear accident have been blamed on errors related to _____ deprivation.

## DOWN

1. It should take about 10–15 _____ to fall asleep. If you always fall asleep faster, you may be sleep deprived.

2. _____ are the only mammal that delay sleep on purpose.

4. While you're asleep, your _____ switches from cleansing your body to rebuilding it.

5. Growth _____, which help the body grow and heal, are released during sleep.

Made in the USA
Middletown, DE
26 September 2023

39275900R10038